T0323029

BRITISH RAIL
DIESELS

BRITISH RAIL
DIESELS

THE LIVES OF THE EARLY DIESELS IN PHOTOGRAPHS

MICK HYMANS

The History Press

First published 2016

The History Press
The Mill, Brimscombe Port
Stroud, Gloucestershire, GL5 2QG
www.thehistorypress.co.uk

© Mick Hymans, 2016

British Library Cataloguing in Publication Data.
A catalogue record for this book is available from the British Library.

ISBN 978 0 7509 6601 6

Typesetting and origination by The History Press
Printed in Great Britain

CONTENTS

PREFACE

My trainspotting days started in the late 1950s when, on my way to junior school, I had to go over the level crossing at Hampden Park – not the one in Glasgow but the first station outside Eastbourne. My mates and I used to watch the 8.20 a.m. pulled by a West Country on its way to Hailsham with a local passenger train. We then hoped it was on time, being due back at 8.55 a.m., before rushing off so we would not be late for the 9 a.m. assembly at school.

Then one day a diesel headed the train. I seem to remember this was greeted with a sense of excitement as we had all copped our first 'D65er', or Class 33 as we came to know them. This initial excitement diminished over time and even led to resentment as our beloved steam engines became increasingly rare.

My home town of Eastbourne did not have too many steam locos with the mainstay of services being in the hands of third-rail electrics – 2 BIL and 2 HAL on Brighton and Hastings services and 6 PUL and 6 PAN running to London. The Cuckoo Line to Tunbridge Wells was not electrified so standard 2-6-4 tanks were a common sight. Saturday mornings saw two expresses to the north of England leave the town, so many Saturday mornings were spent at the end of Platform 1 on Eastbourne Station.

By the time I was 11 years old I was allowed to go to Brighton and by the time I was 14, in 1966, I was travelling all round London with my mates. Sadly by that time the only steam that could be found was at Waterloo, but my Ian Allen combined volume was put to good use nonetheless with Deltics at Kings Cross, Peaks at St Pancras and Westerns at Paddington.

Later, girlfriends, marriage and a young family put my interest on the back burner, but it was while looking through my collection of railway photographs that I was reminded of the number of different classes of diesels there used to be – some more successful than others. Also looking through my collection of railway books, there were books on specific classes of diesel or rail centres but not any that looked at every class. This book, therefore, looks at all the early classes, including the many shunters and prototypes, and has photographs of all the different variations and liveries within the classes. This should be of special interest to modellers wanting to have the correct livery for the period depicted.

A few years ago, diesels were regarded with derision in certain quarters, but as time goes by, those who grew up with diesels are beginning to outnumber the steam enthusiasts. Indeed, some of the preserved railways's most popular days are the special diesel events.

I have compiled this book using mostly my own photographs, acquired over time, but I must thank Grahame Wareham, Keith Long, Charles Verrall and Pete Hackney for use of their collections. I have not knowingly used any images that may be subject to copyright – but if I have, please accept my apologies. If my apologies are not enough, please contact me.

Mick Hymans

SHUNTERS

Apart from a few experimental diesel locomotives, shunters were the first diesels to appear on the rail network. They could be seen at most large stations on empty coaching-stock duties or in every freight yard marshalling wagons. With the loss of freight on the railways and the gradual introduction of diesel multiple units (DMUs) and electric multiple units (EMUs), the need for these small workhorses declined, and these days they can only be spotted at large marshalling yards or diesel depots.

The vast majority were built under British Railways, but there were many classes manufactured by the Big Four prior to nationalisation. Many of these classes only numbered a few in each but many had more than a passing resemblance to the class 03s and 08s, which were built in their hundreds. Many had a 0-6-0 wheel configuration, but there were places where this wheelbase was too long and a shorter 0-4-0 was required. This was usually the case on docksides or industrial estates.

11162 was a Class 05 shunter that became D2559. It was introduced in 1955 after being manufactured by Hunslet and was withdrawn in August 1967. It is seen here at Yarmouth Beach in 1957.

The 04 class of diesel shunter was one of the first classes of diesel locomotives to be built by British Railways after nationalisation in 1948. There were 142 examples built over a ten-year period. They were based on an original design for a one-off shunter introduced in 1948, which worked at Hither Green and had the departmental number DS1173. This was renumbered D2341 in 1967.

Although they were badged as Drewry, the company never had any manufacturing capabilities and the work was subcontracted to Robert Stephenson at the Vulcan Foundry and Hawthorns.

When British Railways took over from the Big Four companies, they devised a numbering system for the diesel locos they acquired and for the planned new additions. Shunters inherited from the London Midland & Scottish Railway (LMS) would be renumbered 13xxx, from the Southern 152xx, from the Great Western Railway (GWR) 151xx and from the London & North Eastern Railway

D2859 was a Class 02 shunter, although it didn't survive long enough to receive an 02 number. It was one of a class of twenty built in 1960–61 to work in areas of restricted loading gauge. Unusually for the UK, they had a door at the rear rather than on either side. They were built by the Yorkshire Engine Company and were powered by a Rolls-Royce engine. This loco was withdrawn in 1969, with the rest of the class disappearing from the network by 1974. Seven of the class have been preserved, but D2859 was scrapped.

Another 0-4-0, D2719, Class D2/10 at Crewe Works in 1965.

D2905 at Devons Road Shed soon after introduction. It was a Class D3/1 0-4-0 shunter made in 1958 by North British. There were fourteen in the class, which survived until 1967. Devons Road (1D) was a rarely photographed shed in Bow, London on the North London Railway. Its claim to fame is that it became the country's first diesel-only depot after closing to steam in 1958. It closed completely in 1964.

11186 (D2409), one of ten Class D2/5s built by Andrew Barclay in 1956–57, spotted on 27 March 1979 at Boston, Lincolnshire. None survived long enough to receive a TOPS classification. 11186 was withdrawn in December 1968.

Class 04 11124 (D2254) at Stewarts Lane Depot in 1958. Note the larger windows and conical chimney that differ from the photograph of 11103 on the next page. The wheels were slightly larger being 3ft 6in as opposed to 3ft 3in.

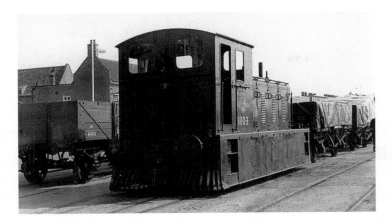

11103, later to become D2203, was seen at Yarmouth in 1957. Introduced in 1952, it was an Class 04 built by Drewry and started her working life on the Wisbech & Upway Tramway. The side skirts and cowcatchers were a legal requirement for any loco running on unfenced street rails. Both Yarmouth Docks and the Wisbech Tramway fall into this category. Four shunters were fitted with these: D2200–D2203. It escaped the cutter's torch and is currently preserved in working order by the Embsay & Bolton Abbey Steam Railway.

Another 04, D2299, photographed at Lincoln in 1961.

Introduced in 1935, this is one of the earliest shunters made for the LMS, one of a batch of ten. It was originally numbered 7074 but was renumbered 12000 in British Railways days. The class was designated D3/6. Seven of the class were sent to France in 1940 to help with the war effort. One example, 7069, survived, was repatriated and is now preserved on the Gloucestershire Warwickshire Railway. It is seen here in 1961 at Derby.

D2597 was a Class 05 manufactured by Hunslet in 1955. Seen here at Ardesley in 1960, it was one of sixty-nine. They were all withdrawn by the end of 1968 but four have been preserved.

D2950 was ordered by British Railways to work specifically on dockside tramways. It was classified D1/1 and was one of three made by Hunslet being introduced in 1954. it is seen here at Ipswich on 19 September 1965. Her two sister engines were cut up in 1967, but D2950 survived until 1983 being used on an industrial site in Llanelli.

No. 87 was built by Barclays in 1958. It is seen here at Thornaby in 1970.

At Stratford on 17 April 1964, this Brush 0-4-0 was snapped. D2999 had a working life of about seven years being introduced on 4 September 1960 and withdrawn on 15 October 1967.

15100, originally numbered 2, was built by Hawthorn Leslie for the GWR as early as 1936. It was classified a D3/10. It was shedded at Swindon, where it was photographed on 6 September 1964. It only lasted another couple of years, being scrapped in 1966.

15215 was built for the Southern Railway for South London marshalling yards. Designed by O.V.S. Bulleid, their wheels bear a resemblance to the wheel design of his West Country/Battle of Britain Pacifics. It was built at Ashford in 1950 and was snapped at Hither Green fourteen years later.

12009 was ordered by the LMS and delivered in 1939. It was an 0-6-0 with very uneven axle spacing. This was due to its having one large traction motor with a jackshaft drive. It is seen at Derby on 7 February 1965. All of the class had been withdrawn by 1967 and none survived into preservation.

ED1, built by Fowlers in 1936, was photographed at Derby on 10 June 1956.

Another Fowlers shunter was ED6, again built in 1936 and seen here at Derby Works.

Designed by Bulleid in 1949 was this six-wheeled shunter. It was built at Ashford Works and lasted ten years before being scrapped in 1959.

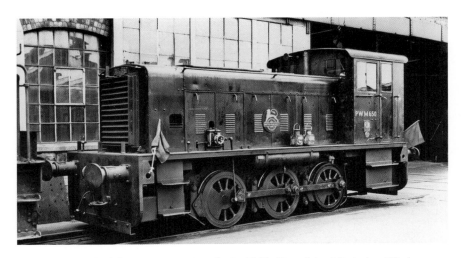

PWM650 was built by Ruston & Hornsby in 1953. Here it is at Swindon Works on 18 August 1955.

11116 (D2500) was built by Hudswell-Clarke in 1956. It was photographed at Derby in 1961. There were only ten of the class built, all of which had been scrapped by 1967.

Photographed at Bradford on 7 July 1968 was D2095 in original British Railways green livery. It was later renumbered 03 195.

Four years later, at Norwich on 24 July 1972, another 03, D2149, has lost the old British Railways symbol and has been adorned with the new double arrow insignia.

(LNER) 150xx. New diesel-mechanical and diesel-hydraulic locos would be numbered 11xxx, while diesel electrics would be 13xxx.

In 1957, the numbering system was changed again as part of the 1955 Modernisation Plan. This change meant that shunting locomotives under 300hp would be given numbers D2000–D2999, while more powerful types with between 300hp and 700hp would be numbered D3000–D4999.

Many of the early shunters first appeared in LMS black unlined livery. After nationalisation in 1948, British Railways green was adopted with a lion-on-wheel emblem. This emblem lasted until 1956, when it was changed to the lion on a crown holding a small wheel.

In 1965 a new corporate identity was launched to try to revitalise the rather staid image of the railways. A new logo – the now famous double arrow – was adopted, together with a striking blue livery, known as Rail Blue.

In 1970 a new Total Operations Processing System (TOPS) was introduced. This was a new computer system brought in from IBM and first used by Southern Pacific Railroad in the USA. It was designed as means of keeping a check on positioning, maintenance, depots and duties of all the company's

A Class 03 in the new blue livery with new number and logo. This was 03 073 at Birkenhead North on 20 August 1987.

03 179 is seen here at Sandown on 10 April 1992 in Network South East livery.

Barclays Class 06 shunter 2423 in Rail Blue livery at Aberdeen Ferryhill Shed on 15 September 1973. It became 06 006 under the TOPS numbering scheme before being scrapped in June 1980.

By the time this photo was taken, 97803 was displaying its fourth number. It started life as 11140, then became D2554, followed by 05 001. It is preserved at Haven Street on the Isle of Wight. The prefix '97' on numbers denoted a departmental locomotive. Seen here at St Johns, Isle of Wight on 31 March 1984.

locomotives. Each class of loco was given a two-digit number, which was followed by a three-digit number for each loco in the class. For some classes the transformation was simple; the 03 locomotives kept the same last three digits, so D2149 became 03 149. Not all classes followed this rule, so life must have been a trifle confusing for the poor trainspotters of the period!

The 03 shunters were probably the most successful class of small diesel shunters, with 230 built at British Railways workshops in Swindon and Doncaster. They were introduced between 1957 and 1962, and the early ones were numbered 11187–11209 (D2000–D2022), being introduced before the new numbering system of the time. They were to be seen in marshalling yards all over the country as well as acting as station pilots. They were even used on a few passenger workings. Perhaps the most famous of these was to pull the boat trains through the streets of Weymouth on to the quay.

As reasons for this type of engine being built gradually disappeared then so did the locos, and the class was withdrawn from 1968 onwards. Only sixty-eight of these survived to be listed in Ian Allen's 1978 *British Railways Locoshed Book*. By 1987 they had disappeared from mainland services but two survived on the Isle of Wight and in private industry. Fifty-five have survived into preservation

Class 08 D3051 in British Railways green livery, captured at Derby in May 1963.

Another shot of an 08, this time at Cardiff. 08 652 passes on a parcels train.

The Class 08 shunter was the most abundant type of loco, with 996 produced. They were to be seen at stations and goods yards nationwide. Based on the ex-LMS 12xxx series, they started appearing on the network in 1952. Like the 03s, the first examples were introduced bearing the older numbering system: D3000–D3336 first appeared as 13000–13336. Production of the class ceased in 1962, having kept British Railways works busy at Derby, Crewe, Darlington, Horwich and Doncaster for ten years.

The first 08 was withdrawn from service in 1967, with most of the class meeting a similar fate over the next few years. But around 100 are still being used by rail operators around the country. There are over sixty examples that have been preserved and most heritage railways now benefit from this versatile locomotive.

There was a very similar class, the 09s, that differed from the 08s only in the gearing. There were only twenty-six of this class produced, all of which were allocated to the Southern Region. The difference in gearing meant that they had a slightly higher top speed at the expense of tractive effort. Introduced between 1959 and 1962, in later years many of the 08s were converted to 09s. They have occasionally been spotted on passenger trains working from

08 754 on 8 July 1954, looking very smart at Eastleigh, possibly just after a repaint.

08 668 at Cardiff on 9 May 1984.

It is 21 March 1987 and 09 005 poses at Clapham Junction, with a Class 73 in the background on a parcels train.

D2988 was a Class 07 working on Southampton Docks in 1963.

Clapham Junction to Kensington Olympia when filling in for a failed Class 33. Ten have been preserved, including 09 018 on the Bluebell Railway.

There were fourteen Class 07 shunters produced by Ruston & Hornsby in 1962. They were unusual in being built with an off-centre cab. They all suffered very badly from overheating axle boxes when travelling long distances. In fact, the very first one suffered from this while being delivered. Luckily they were built to replace the USA steam locos employed at Southampton Docks, which involved very little running. If they needed to be worked on, a fitter had to be sent from Eastliegh or they had to suffer the ignominy of being transported by road. Three were cut up at Eastleigh before they could receive TOPS 07 numbers. Most of the others were bought by private companies after British Railways had finished with them. Six are currently at preserved railways, but not all are in good working order.

Strictly speaking, the Class 14 locos should not be classified as shunters. They were originally designed to work freights between local yards over short distances, but with their centre cabs and dual controls, they lent themselves

Class 14 D9544 at Swindon on 29 May 1965.

admirably to shunting duties. The original order of twenty-six was increased to fifty-six before the first one was even built. The last in the series to be built, D9555, was also the last ever locomotive to be built at Swindon Works. They had a very short working life and, as with most other shunters, they were being withdrawn by the late 1960s. Many found work in industry.

In 2005, D9504 was leased from its preservation owners to work once more on the network. It was employed during the construction of High Speed 1 around St Pancras, where it was in charge of the twenty-two-wagon concrete pumping train. Five were exported and nineteen have been preserved and can sometimes be seen on light passenger workings.

EXPERIMENTAL LOCOMOTIVES

Co-Co 10000 at Derby in 1960.

Locomotives 10000 and 10001 were the first main-line diesels to operate on the railways in Britain. They were ordered by the LMS and built at Derby. No. 10000 was introduced in November 1947 and outshopped in the LMS black livery that had been used for their shunters. No. 10001, however, did not appear until July 1948, after nationalisation, and was therefore painted in British Railways green livery. They were designed by H.G. Ivatt, who ignored British Railways' instruction to remove the LMS lettering from 10000, and the lettering stayed until after Ivatt's retirement in 1951. 10000 was presented to the press in December 1947 at Euston Station, from where it made a demonstration return run to Watford.

They were powered by an English Electric 1600hp diesel engine with electric transmission. They started revenue-earning service by operating passenger trains from St Pancras and Euston, but lacked the power to comfortably handle fully loaded express trains. Operating together on 1 June 1949, however, they managed to pull the Royal Scot non-stop from Euston to Glasgow with a sixteen-carriage, 545-ton load, returning to London the following day with the southbound service. They continued to operate in tandem until later in 1949, from when they were used individually between London and the north of England or Scottish destinations. Occasionally they were used on freight services between Willesden and the north.

In March 1953, No. 10000 and 10001 were transferred to the Southern Region so comparisons could be made with Bulleid's 10201-3. They worked expresses out of Waterloo, including the Bournemouth Belle. They returned to the LMS in 1955 ; they were both overhauled at Derby and then continued to work north of England expresses including The Royal Scot.

They were both withdrawn in 1963 and stored at Derby. No. 10001 was put back into traffic, complete with yellow front panels where it worked freights and the occasional express from North London. Between them they achieved a combined total of over 2,000,000 miles. Despite some attempts by railwaymen to save the locos, and an offer of £10,000 to Clapham Railway Museum that was declined as it did not have enough space and the locomotive did not represent a class, 10000 was cut up at Cashmores in 1968. No. 10001 suffered a similar fate earlier that year at Cox & Danks. There is now a group,

10001 in British Railways green livery having had yellow panel added seen at Willesden in 1965.

the Ivatt Diesel Recreation Society, dedicated to building a replica of the class and it has acquired an original engine.

Loco number 10800 was ordered by the LMS in 1946 but not delivered until 1950. It was designed by H.G. Ivatt as a replacement for steam on secondary and branch lines. It was the forerunner of British Railways' Class 15 and 16 locos. It remained in service until 1959 and was sold to Brush in 1962 where it was finally broken up in 1972.

Perhaps the ugliest and most radical diesel ever constructed was 10100. It was known as the Fell Locomotive as it was a joint venture between Lieutenant Colonel L.F.R. Fell, Davy Paxman & Co. Ltd and Shell Refining & Marketing Co. Ltd. It was another of Ivatt's designs and was built at the LMS works at Derby in 1950, where it was trialled the following year. It had a 4-8-4 wheel arrangement with the eight centre wheels being coupled. This was later altered into a 4-4+4-4 wheel arrangement. It also boasted six diesel engines, four of which were used for traction and the other two were used

10001 on shed at Willesden on 27 July 1962. (Charles Verrall)

Bo-Bo 10800 pictured at Derby in 1958, and below, another view at the same location.

to power auxiliary services such as pressure chargers and fans. The reasoning behind having four engines was that if one or more failed the loco could still continue its journey using the others. It also meant that the weight could be distributed and a lighter chassis used. When it was introduced it was the most powerful locomotive in the country, with a power output of 2,000bhp and a tractive effort of 25,000lbf.

Originally appearing with the LMS black livery and a silver stripe, in 1955 10100 was repainted in British Railway's green livery. It spent much of its revenue-earning life on passenger trains between London, Derby and

Manchester. Depending on the source of information, its demise was caused either by a fire at Manchester or by a major gearbox failure after surviving the fire. Most sources agree that it was withdrawn in 1958 and was scrapped in 1960 at Derby.

D0280 was built by Brush at their factory at Loughborough. It was designed as a second-generation lightweight Class 4 diesel electric locomotive. As no single lightweight engine powerful enough existed, it utilised two German Maybach MD655 engines, as had been used in the Class 52 Western series.

In 1952 Eastbourne hosted the International Union of Railways Conference as well as an exhibition of locos, which was held in the goods yard. 10100 was one of the exhibits. (Charles Verrall)

D0280 Falcon at the Brush Works in 1961.

These engines were manufactured in the UK under licence by Bristol Siddeley. The major difference between D0280 and the Westerns was that the former used electric-traction motors rather than hydraulic ones.

Originally outshopped in September 1961, D0280 bore a lime green and chestnut livery. It was briefly based at Finsbury Park before being transferred to the Western Region. It was not given the nameplate *Falcon* until it returned to Brush in 1962 for an overhaul. It returned to service briefly in 1963 but was then shedded in Sheffield before once again being taken out of service. It did, however, put in another appearance in the standard British Railways livery with yellow ends, but by now Brush had developed a single lightweight engine of comparable power, which was to be used in the Class 47s. The writing was on the wall for *Falcon*.

It returned to the Western Region at Bristol Bath Road, where together with the Westerns, it could be seen working expresses to Paddington and to Ebbw Vale, where it worked iron-ore trains. In 1970 British Railways purchased the locomotive from Brush for about its scrap value. It was overhauled at Swindon Works, re-emerging in Rail Blue livery with full yellow ends. British Railways designated it a Class 53 and renumbered it 1200. It was withdrawn in 1975 and cut up at Cashmores in May 1976 after having covered more than 635,000 miles.

D0260 *Lion* was created in 1962 by the Birmingham Railway Carriage & Wagon Company (BRC&W) in order to demonstrate to British Railways the type of Type-4 diesel locomotive they were capable of building. It was powered by a 2,750hp Sulzer engine capable of 100mph. It took part in several tests in July and August 1962 including making a standing start up the Lickey Incline with a load of sixteen coaches weighing 519 tons reaching a speed of 20mph at the summit. A further test with twenty coaches weighing 639 tons was successful when a speed of 17mph was attained. It was officially handed over to British Railways at a ceremony at Marylebone on 28 May.

Lion was first used on revenue-earning service when it hauled the 7.25 a.m. on 14 May 1962 from Wolverhampton to Paddington. It was shedded at Wolverhampton, probably because this was the closest to where it was built at BRC&W works at Smethwick. It continued hauling expresses out of Paddington to the Midlands for a short while, but was then moved to Finsbury Park Shed, where it was put in charge of expresses out of Kings Cross.

It had a very short but useful life, as British Railways decided that Brush would get the order for their Type-4 locomotives in the shape of the Class 47s.

D0280 *Falcon* awaits departure from Paddington.

D0260 *Lion* on the Yorkshire Pullman passing Newark on 12 September 1963.

0260 *Lion* heads the Yorkshire Pullman out of Leeds Central. (Charles Verrall)

Indeed, an order for the first twenty Brush Type-4s (D1500–D1519) had been placed before the trials of *Lion* were even completed. It was withdrawn from service in January 1964 when it was discovered that the engine had a cracked sump. It was stripped for parts and the engine was allegedly used in a Class 47 loco. After all useful electrics and components were taken from it, the body went to T.W. Ward for scrap.

Without a healthy order book and with their bankers foreclosing on their loans, the BRC&W Co. was forced to downsize and the North Works at Smethwick was closed with all further production focused at its South Works. The only order it had was for underground stock and this was subsequently handed over to Metropolitan Cammell. Thereafter the company ceased railway production.

The original Deltic was numbered DP1 (Diesel Prototype No. 1) but this was never applied to the locomotive. It was built by Dick, Kerr & Co. of Preston, in 1955. The order was placed by English Electric, which incorporated the engine manufacturer Napier & Sons. Its engines were two down-rated versions of a 1750hp engine fitted to minesweepers. The 1650hp version fitted to the locos was designed to decrease stress and lead to a longer life. Although the engine was going to be named *Enterprise*, Hudswell Clarke beat them to it on a range of their engines. *Deltic* was painted in a pale blue livery with cream stripes along the sides and chevrons on the front. The headlight on the front was not fitted to later locomotives. It started trials on freight services between London and Liverpool and the following year on the Settle–Carlisle Line.

Deltic passes Doncaster on 11 April 1959.

Another shot of *Deltic*, this time passing Newark on 20 June 1959.

The chief mechanical engineer of the London Midland Region was not a supporter of high-revving diesel engines and declined to invest in further examples. If it had not been for the Eastern Region looking for powerful engines to replace the express steam locomotives on the Kings Cross to Newcastle and Edinburgh routes, no more would have been produced.

Gerald Fiennes, the traffic manager at the time, overcame objections to investing in a fleet of Deltics. These objections included a limited top speed due to their weight and the need to alter platforms at Kings Cross due to their size. Twenty-two were ordered to replace fifty-five steam locos (see Class 55).

At first glance one could be forgiven for thinking that DP2 was a variation of the Deltic Class. It was built by the same manufacturer on the Deltic production line, but it was radically different. It only had one engine – an

Deltic on a freight at Newark on 17 March 1959.

DP2 at Newark alongside WD 2-8-0 90700 in December 1963.

English Electric 2,700hp unit that gave a top speed of 90mph. It was later modified to have electronic control systems and was, in fact, the forerunner of the much-loved Class 50 locos. DP2 made its debut run on 2 May 1962, when it ran light from Newton-le-Willows to Chester and back. Later that month it was pulling express trains from Euston and later from Kings Cross.

After being overhauled in 1965, the original Brunswick green livery was replaced to match the Deltic two-tone green colour scheme and was often to be seen on the Sheffield Pullman. Despite not having the same power as the Deltics, it was fitted with traction control, which gave it superior acceleration and it was more than capable of being used on Deltic duties. In 1967 it was involved in an accident at Thirsk, where it hit a derailed cement train. The front end suffered damage so severe that it was not economical to repair and it was withdrawn. Its engine was used in a Class 50 – either D400 or D417 depending on which source you read.

Nos 10201, 2 and 3 were diesel locomotives built for the Southern Region in the early 1950s. They were designed by O.V.S. Bulleid prior to nationalisation but not built until later. Nos 10201 and 10202 were introduced in 1951 after

10201 as new before the British Railways emblems were applied.

10203 spotted at Derby Works on 20 June 1962.

being built at Ashford Works, and 10203 was built about three years later at Brighton Works. They were powered by English Electric engines and were capable of 110mph before the gear ratios were altered to make them suitable for freight traffic as well as passenger duties.

Their time on the Southern Region came to an end when they were transferred to the London Midland Region and were based at Willesden. Being non-standard they were withdrawn in 1963 and were stored at Derby before being cut up at Cashmores in 1968.

HS4000 *Kestrel* was another experimental locomotive designed in 1967. British Railways wanted a new Type-5 diesel producing over 3,000bhp and weighing under 126 tons. It had to be capable of hauling passenger and freight services. Brush responded with HS4000, which was powered by a single 16-cylinder Sulzer engine. It was painted in a livery of yellow ochre over chocolate brown with the two colours being separated by a thin white line. It was officially handed over at Marylebone Station on 29 January 1968. Its power was ably demonstrated by pulling twenty Mk1 carriages over Shap, reaching the summit at 46mph. It was equally impressive with freight trains, pulling one coal train weighing 2,028 tons between Mansfield and Lincoln.

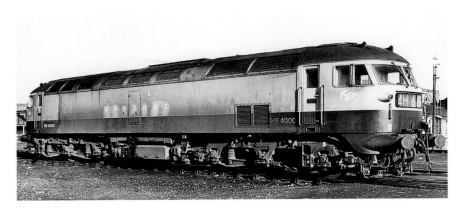

HS4000 *Kestrel* at Hull on 14 April 1969.

HS4000 *Kestrel* at Marylebone on 29 January 1968 prior to hauling a special press test train.

The thirty-two-hopper train was the heaviest train ever to operate on British Railways. The axle weight was over the 20-ton limit set by British Railways so it was re-bogied, meaning it had less power, but it still took fourteen minutes off the time of a Kings Cross–Newcastle service normally in the hands of Deltics.

It was withdrawn from service in 1971 and sold to Russia for £127,000, leaving these shores via Cardiff Docks.

CLASS 15

There were forty-four of these Type-1 diesel electric locomotives built. Type-1 meant that they had a power output of less than 1,000bhp. They were one of the first main-line diesels to be ordered by British Railways – the first being introduced in 1957, with the rest being delivered over the next four years. They were designed by British Houston-Thomson, built by the Yorkshire Engine Company and Clayton Equipment Company, and they used Paxman engines. A good example of just how many companies collaborated in the building of these locos.

The original order was for ten locomotives (D8200–D8209) and these were built by the Yorkshire Engine Company. They proved to be successful and a further thirty-four were ordered (D8210–D8243). These were built at Claytons in Derbyshire.

D8205 at Devons Road in 1958.

43

D8242, in green livery but with the double arrow logo, at Stratford in April 1970. (G. Wareham)

Devons Road Depot at Bow East London was allotted the first ten. This was so that their performance could be compared with other Type-1s that were being produced at the time by North British (Class 16) and English Electric (Class 20).

The entire class soon found their way over to East London, being shedded at Stratford (30A) and Finsbury Park (34G), with some venturing as far as Ipswich (32B). They were designed for freight and empty coaching-stock working. Dogged by expensive engine problems, together with poor visibility from the cabs and being few in number, the future was not bright for these engines. A decision to withdraw the class was taken in the late 1960s and they had all gone from revenue-earning service by April 1971. Four survived to be used as electric train heating units. Three of these units, numbered DB968000/2/3, lasted another ten years before being broken up. The fourth, DB986001 (D8233), has been preserved.

D8201 at Devons Road, Bow, in October 1959. (G. Wareham)

Just out of the paint shop and still in green livery but with the double arrow adorning its side and missing the 'D', 8234 was snapped at Liverpool Street in April 1970. (G. Wareham)

CLASS 16

The Class 16 Type-1 diesel locomotives must rank as one of the least successful classes in British Railway history. There were only ten produced and these were trialled against the Class 15s and 20s, which were built at the same time. They bore a resemblance to the Class 15s and shared the same Paxman engine, but suffered from ventilation and overheating problems.

They were all built by the North British Locomotive Company at their plant in Glasgow and delivered to Devons Road (1D) before being moved on to Stratford (30A), where they spent most of their short working lives on local freight traffic. They were withdrawn in 1968 and scrapped before any possibility of preservation.

D8409 at Stratford, where it spent most of its working life. (G. Wareham)

Awaiting the cutter's torch at Kettering are D8401 (above) with full yellow end and D8405 (below) with small yellow warning panel. None of the class received indicator panels, but they retained the route indicator discs. (G. Wareham)

CLASS 17

The Class 17s were built by Beyer, Peacock & Co. of Manchester and the Claytons Equipment Company of Hatton in Derbyshire, hence the nickname 'Claytons'. There were 117 produced between 1962 and 1965. Claytons produced models D8500–D8587, while D8588–D8616 were built by Beyer, Peacock & Co. The design had a central cab with a Paxman six-cylinder engine on either side, each generating 450bhp – making them Type-1s. Two of the class, D8586 and D8587, were fitted with eight-cylinder Rolls-Royce engines that generated the same power.

The central cab with lower bonnets was supposed to give better visibility than the Class 15 and 16s, which had a single cab at one end.

D8549 on shed at Motherwell (66B) on 6 April 1969.

D8560 at Worcester (85A) in June 1969. (G. Wareham)

D8521 at Derby Railway Technical Centre (RTC) in July 1970. (G. Wareham)

D8583 heads a line of similar diesels at Millerhill (64B). (G. Wareham)

The entire class was eventually allocated to Scottish depots, but not before undergoing some unsuccessful trials around the north-east, which included double-heading on iron ore trains from Consett – even two locos could not handle these heavy trains. It proved to be one of the shortest-lived of all classes due to unreliability – some of them only lasted five years. Withdrawal started in the late 1960s and they had all disappeared from the network by 1975. A few were purchased by private operators.

D8521 and D8598 enjoyed a brief reprieve at the Derby Research Centre; one as a mobile power plant and the other on test trains. Both were eventually withdrawn in 1978 and subsequently scrapped. D8568 made it into preservation after it had been used by private operators including Hemelite of Hemel Hempstead and Ribblesdale Cement of Clitheroe.

CLASS 20

The first of the Class 20 diesel-electric locomotives was introduced in 1957 and production continued for the next eleven years, with 228 examples being made. Manufactured by English Electric and the Vulcan Foundry, numbering D8000–D8199 and D8300–D8327, they were Type-1 engines, which meant they had between 800 and 1000bhp. They became known as 'choppers' by trainspotters of the period due to the noise made by the locos when working hard, which resembled a helicopter.

They were built as light mixed-traffic locos, but were rarely seen on passenger work. As more and more light-freight traffic was being transferred to the roads much of their work dried up.

D8129 at Crewe on 13 February 1966 soon after its introduction.

Their design was unusual for diesels made for use in the UK, as they only had one cab. This led to visibility problems for the crews when travelling nose first. To alleviate this problem, they were often seen working in pairs joined at the noses, so they had a cab at either end. This also meant that the combined power output was 2000bhp, so that hauling heavy freights at speeds of up to 75mph was possible.

The first twenty-eight locos were equipped with steam-engine-style disc indicators, but later locos had headcode boxes fitted. They were originally allocated to the Eastern and Scottish Regions with depots at Devons Road, Hornsey, Norwich, Tinsley, Eastfield and Haymarket all receiving some. Locomotives used in the Highlands of Scotland had tablet-catcher recesses fitted beneath cab windows. Some Class 20s found themselves south of the capital when they were used in the construction of the Channel Tunnel and High Speed 1. They have also been used on weedkiller trains.

In 1966 D8048 was given an all-over Rail Blue livery as part of British Rail's design team experiments. This livery included blue roof and buffer beams but had an all-yellow front end and black under frames. D8078 was the first of the class to be delivered in this livery. Later liveries include Railfreight, British Rail Telecommunications and Direct Rail Services. Most have now been withdrawn, but those that remain and are still used singly have had video cameras fitted to the fronts to aid visibility.

Twenty-seven Class 20s have survived into preservation.

D8008 was one of the first of the class to be introduced and assigned to Devons Road Depot in East London. The brackets for holding the discs can be seen above the buffers.

The recess for accepting a tablet can be seen beneath the cab window of 8113, photographed at 60A Inverness on 15 September 1973. This was another of the class fitted with discs rather than an indicator box.

Just after being outshopped from Crewe Works, D8323 is sporting Rail Blue livery and the double arrow symbol whilst retaining its original number.

20202 captured in Rail Blue livery at Ayr Shed on 23 August 1986.

20137 *Murray B. Hofmeyr* sporting Railfreight livery at Thornaby on 31 July 1988.

Direct rail services gave some Class 20s another lease of life when they were used to transport flasks of nuclear waste from Dungeness Power station in Kent to the nuclear processing site at Sellafield. Above 20309/20310 await their next trip on 25 February 1999, while below 20302/20303 pass beneath the loading gantry at Dungeness on 25 June 1999.

CLASS 21

D6104 at Newark in 1959. It was originally shedded at Hornsey (34B) before being reassigned to Eastfield Glasgow (65A) from April 1960. One of its last duties was as a banker up the Cowlairs Incline at Glasgow. This incline varied between 1 in 41.5 and 1 in 50. D6104 was withdrawn in December 1967.

Introduced between 1958–60, these North British Type-2 diesel electrics were classified as Class 21, despite the fact that none of them survived long enough to bear the TOPS numbering system. The original order was for ten diesel electric locomotives, largely for evaluation against locomotives produced by Brush, the BRC&W Co. and English Electric. Further orders were placed and in total fifty-eight of the class were introduced.

The first thirty-eight were assigned to the Eastern Region at Stratford, Hornsey and Ipswich and used on commuter services into London. Within a couple of years they were all transferred to Eastfield Depot in Scotland;

D6122 at Woodhams scrapyard at Barry Island on 13 October 1968. It survived until 1980 when it was cut up. (Pete Hackney)

D6154 on a whisky train from Elgin passes the Speyburn Distillery near Rothes.

D6152 after finishing shunting pulls a freight train out of Rothes.

D6114 at St Rollox on 30 June 1966 with destination panel and larger yellow warning panel.

D6123, without the route indicator box and small yellow warning panel, at Dundee on 28 June 1966.

they suffered from high failure rates, and this depot was the closest to the manufacturer's factory where they could be returned for repair under warranty. The North British Locomotive Company closed in 1962.

Constant engine problems with the class meant that twenty of them were fitted with Paxman Ventura engines. They also had the old-style steam headcode discs replaced by four-character indicator blinds. These were reclassified as Class 29s. They were used on local freight and passenger services over much of Scotland, sometimes double-headed on express services. The entire class was withdrawn by the end of 1968 and none have survived into preservation.

CLASS 22

D6322 at Teignmouth on 18 August 1963. It was withdrawn in May 1971.

Fifty-eight of these locomotives – known as 'Baby Warships' – were built for the Western Region. The first was delivered in 1959 with the rest following over the next three years and were used primarily on local passenger and freight services in the West Country, although some found their way to Paddington for use on empty coaching stock duties. They were Type-2 diesel hydraulics produced by the North British Locomotive Co. which ceased trading in 1962. From the middle of the 1960s, spares were becoming difficult to source and some engines were cannibalised to keep others working.

D6329, with destination panels and yellow panel added at either side, on 3 October 1968.

Initially they appeared in a green livery with a grey band around the lower bodywork. From 1967 they started appearing in Rail Blue livery, with the first four repaints having yellow panels, and subsequent repaints having full yellow ends. Although they proved to be fairly reliable, they were not as powerful as the Hymeks and Warships. The first of the class was withdrawn in 1967, with the last disappearing in 1971. None survived into preservation.

CLASS 23

D5901 at Derby on 28 September 1969.

There were ten Class 23s produced in 1959. Their introduction was not without problems, however, as they were later found to be overweight. The Bo-Bos had to go through a lightening exercise, which involved making circular holes in the bogie frames and replacing steel buffer beams and roof panels with lighter aluminium ones. After they finally reached the required weight, they were accepted by British Railways and allocated to Doncaster, where they entered service in the spring of 1959.

Utilising half-sized versions of the Napier engine installed in the Deltics, their shorter length gave rise to the nickname 'Baby Deltics'. They proved

D5905 at Doncaster Works in 1963, before receiving a yellow panel and having its doors welded and a destination panel fitted. (G. Wareham)

D5909 in Rail Blue at Hitchin in July 1970. (G. Wareham)

What a difference a year makes! D5909 again, here at
Stratford (30A) on 29 August 1971.

to be unreliable, with cylinder linings frequently cracking and the auxiliary
gearbox, which drove the compressor, being prone to failure. By the end of
1960, the ten locomotives had undergone forty-four engine changes.

They had been delivered in a green livery and numbered D5900–D5909.
Like other early diesels, they were built with nose doors, which became
redundant after a while. These were welded up and destination indicators
added to the fronts. Some of the class received full yellow ends, but only one
made it into Rail Blue livery – D5909.

By 1963 they were based at Finsbury Park and worked out of Kings Cross
on outer-suburban services. Being small in number, the class were regarded as
non-standard by the end of the decade and began to be withdrawn in 1968.
It took three years before the last of the class disappeared. D5901 did linger
on at the Railway Technical Centre until 1975, being cut up two years later.
None have been preserved.

CLASS 24

D5035 passing through Harrow & Wealdstone with a down train on 19 August 1961. (Charles Verrall)

There were 151 of these Class 24 locos produced. They were originally numbered D5000–D5150 and introduced from 1958 onwards. D5000 was presented to the British Transport Commission (BTC) at Marylebone on 24 July before it headed off to its home shed, Crewe South (5B). It is sometimes forgotten that steam engines were still being produced and 9Fs 92233/4/5 were allocated to the Western Region at the same time.

24072 at Doncaster in November 1977.

In 1959, due to delays in the electrification scheme, D5000–D5006 were shedded at Hither Green prior to the first of the Class 33s being delivered. They were then discovered to be too heavy for some lines and had to have their boilers removed.

Apart from D5000, the first engines to be delivered sported an all-over green livery with a wide white stripe at solebar level. Later locomotives appeared with a yellow rectangle at either end, and then all over yellow ends. There were variations to a few in the series – some were fitted with headcode boxes and Inverness-based locomotives had after-market car headlights fitted to aid visibility on sharply curved branch lines.

They could be spotted throughout most of the country north of London, and one of the more famous turns it was rostered on was the Condor freight service between London and Glasgow. They were in charge of this from 1961 when they took over from the Metrovicks. They were also in charge of a second Condor service that ran from Aston, Birmingham to Glasgow. The Condor ran until 1965 when it was replaced by the freightliner service.

The Class 24s were equally at home on freight and passenger duties being used double-headed on iron-ore trains in the north-east and singly on

24001 awaiting the end at Doncaster on 6 November 1977.

ADB968008 (24054) at March in April 1983. It had been used for train heating purposes at Newton Abbot until October 1982. 24054 was withdrawn in August and became TDB968008, being allocated to Newton Abbot until finally withdrawn in October 1982.

D5054 repainted in its original livery at Crewe Works in December 1987. It has been preserved and can be seen on the East Lancashire Railway.

97 201 (D5061, 24061 and RDB968007) is pictured here at Worksop Open Day on 6 June 1987. In November 1975, it was transferred to British Railways' research department at Derby Works, and was allocated the number RDB968007. This loco was subsequently renumbered 97201 and was finally withdrawn in 1987.

passenger services from Inverness through the Scottish Highlands. D5096 was the first diesel to be built at Darlington Works; it was delivered in 1960.

In October 1969, traffic had increased in the Eastern Region and their fleet was not enough to handle the extra work. Five of the Type-2s kept in storage by the London Midland Region were put back into service. These were 5000, 5001, 5013, 5018 and 5090. Early in 1978, two rail tours were run with 24082 and 24087 in charge. They hauled the Merseyside Express from St Pancras to Liverpool and back. 24087 and 24133 hauled the Cambrian Coast Express from Birmingham to Barmouth. However, 24087 failed on this trip and never worked again.

By 1979 only three of the class remained in service: 24061, 24081 and 24082. 24081 survived the longest and was not withdrawn until October 1980. Fourteen of the class did not last long enough to receive their TOPS number. Four of the class have been preserved.

24 035 at Doncaster Works on 7 January 1979.

D5071 passing Finsbury Park with a cross-London freight on 12 June 1962.
(Charles Verrall)

CLASS 25

The Class 25s were more powerful versions of the Class 24s. It became evident that a top speed of 75mph was not good enough and the increase in horsepower of the Class 25s meant an increase in top speed to 90mph. A total of 327 Class 25s were built, with the first eighty-two (D5151–D5232 and 25001–25082) being visibly similar to the Class 24s except for the addition of a route indicator box above the cabs. The first of the class was introduced in 1961, and it was six years before the last in the class appeared.

25062 was one of the earlier Class 25s. It had originally been built with doors at the front to enable crews to change engines if double-heading, but they had been welded up to help prevent draughts and reduce noise. It is pictured here at Warrington on 16 May 1982.

From D5233 the main differences to the bodywork centred on the cabs. The doors at the front, which allowed access between two locos when double-heading, were rarely used and were a source of draughts within the cab; they were therefore discontinued. This meant that a larger centre window could be fitted. The air intakes were also moved to the roof from the body sides. They were also delivered bearing two-tone green paintwork.

Although the locos were primarily designed for freight work, they were used on some passenger services. This meant that boilers had to be fitted to those engines for train heating purposes.

They were mainly built at British Railway's works at Darlington and Derby. Some of the later locos were contracted out to Beyer, Peacock and Company, but the company ran into financial problems and the final eighteen were built at British Railways's Derby Works. They appeared on most of the country's lines, but the Eastern and Southern Regions were not allocated any.

D5236 (25086), in new-style two-tone green livery and with redesigned cab, at Derby in early 1964.

25 185 at Toton on 10 March 1985.

25 288 at Crewe Station on 15 February 1987.

25 912 was one of twelve Class 25s designated 25/9. It was intended that these twelve engines would be used on freight that was won for the Industrial Minerals Division. This included salt for road gritting from the mine at Winsford, Cheshire. As it turned out, they were displaced by Class 31s.

97252 (25314) *Ethel 3* at Bletchley on 28 March 1987.

97251 (25305) *Ethel 2* at Perth Station on 23 May 1986.

25048 double-heading with 25200 on a train of tankers on 31 May 1984 at Chester.

They acquired two nicknames. To trainspotters they were known as 'rats', as they could be seen everywhere and were as common as vermin. Train crews had another name for them, 'Spluts', as this was the noise they made when they broke down – a frequent occurence!

Three Class 25/3s were converted into mobile generators to provide electric heating on passenger trains where the hauling locomotive was not able to supply heat. They were numbered 97250/1/2 (formally 25310/25305/25314). They were also known as *Ethel 1*, *2* and *3*, with Ethel standing for Electric Train Heating Ex Locomotives. They were painted in the same livery as the coaching stock they were coupled to and were withdrawn between 1987 and 1990.

Twenty of the class have been preserved.

25042 and 25224 head a passenger train out of Birmingham New Street on 26 May 1984.

CLASS 26

D5325 (26 025) at Perth on 28 June 1966.

5330 (26030) in Rail Blue livery outside Inverness Shed on
15 September 1973.

5335 (26035) clearly showing the recess beneath the cab for catching the tablet on single-line working pictured at Aberdeen (Ferryhill 61B) on 15 September 1973.

26 029 with front corner damage alongside 25911 at Carlisle Shed on 21 June 1986.

There were forty-seven Class 26 locomotives built by the BRC&W Co. at their Smethwick Works, introduced in 1958 and 1959. The BRC&W Co. had been a manufacturer of rolling stock and diesel multiple units, but in 1957 they produced twelve diesel locos for the Irish railways (CIE101 Class). The company used Sulzer engines from Switzerland to power their locomotives.

At the time British Railways were evaluating different engines from a variety of manufacturers and BRC&W Co. was awarded an initial order to build twenty Type-2 mixed-traffic locomotives. They were initially delivered to Hornsey Traction Maintenance Depot (34B) and were compared with diesels manufactured by English Electric, North British Locomotive Company, Brush and British Railways' own workshops. The second batch (D5320–D5346) was delivered to Scotland, being shedded at Haymarket (64B). After the evaluation trials were over, the entire class was allocated to Scotland with Haymarket and Inverness receiving the lion's share.

26025 in Freight Grey rail livery, large double arrow emblem and all-round yellow ends and black window surrounds at Princess Street Gardens on 25 August 1986.

After the end of steam in 1968, the 'D' was removed from the numbers on loco sides. They could be seen on the picturesque line to the Kyle of Lochalsh as well as the main line north and south of Inverness. They were also rostered on the the Royal Highlander, which was the sleeper service to Euston. They were in charge of this service as far as Perth and it needed three locomotives working in multiple to operate.

Although some Class 37s and 47s were allocated to the area, the reliability of the class extended their lives. They were given overhauls during the 1980s. In 1987 most of the engines were allocated to Eastfield (65A) until 1992 when they were allocated to Inverness (60A) but by now they were nearly expired being around 35 years old. It had been envisaged that many of the class would last until 2000, but the closure of Ravenscraig Steelworks had a significant effect and the last example was withdrawn in 1993. Thirteen of the class have been preserved

CLASS 27

The original loco in the class, D5300, had been renumbered 26 007. It was repainted and renumbered into its original livery and is seen at Thornaby (51L) on 20 September 1992.

The Class 27s were a development of the Class 26s. They were introduced in 1961–62 and numbered sixty-nine in total. The number sequence followed straight on from the Class 26s – D5347–D5415. They had 90bhp more power but weighed 5 tons less than the Class 26s.

Some of the diesels were temporarily allocated to the London area, working Tilbury boat trains and cross-London freights, but all of the class gradually worked their way north and by the end of 1969 they were all allocated to Scotland. They replaced the Clayton Class 17s that were proving very

27 104 at Derby Works in November 1982. This was one of the locos that had been converted to push-pull working for the Edinburgh Waverley–Glasgow Queen Street service.

27 007 and 47 017 bring a passenger train into Inverness Station on 5 July 1984.

A row of Class 27s headed by 27 004 to the fore. Behind it are 20 017,012, 010,004, 007.

unreliable. One of the services they could be seen on was the Edinburgh Waverley–Glasgow Queen Street, which had been operated by ageing Inter-City DMUs that were becoming increasingly unreliable. Some were converted for push–pull operation and reclassified as Class 27/1; others had electric heating installed and were classified as 27/2, topping and tailing the intercity expresses with one of the class at either end. The 27/2s were prone to catching fire with their train heating alternators being the source of most fires.

They were superseded in 1980 by Class 47s. In 1987 many were withdrawn following the discovery of blue asbestos and they had all disappeared before the older, slower-revving, more reliable Class 26s. Eight of the class have been preserved.

27 203 (D5393, 27 121) languishes at Derby on 3 December 1983. The damage at the front was due to a collision near Glasgow when pulling a rake of oil wagons. It ran into the back of a Class 303 electric unit at Dalmuir Station on 14 September 1982. It was cut up in 1986.

27066 at Eastfield Shed (65A) on 24 August 1986.

27 056 at Eastfield Shed in July 1984 looking in very good condition and sporting a white band along the bottom of the sides. The loco had been spruced up to haul a royal train carrying Prince Charles from Glasgow to Fort William on 20 November 1983.

CLASS 28

The Class 28s were unique in this country as they had a Co-Bo wheel arrangement – three axles at one end and two at the other. There were twenty examples built in 1958 by Metropolitan Vickers – hence the nickname Metrovicks.

They were all assigned to the London Midland Region but by mid 1963 had all been reallocated to Barrow Depot, where they finished their working days. They suffered engine problems from the outset and in 1961 the whole class were handed back to the manufacturers to remedy the problems.

D5710 on shed at Barrow (12E) in February 1959. (Keith Long)

One of the duties that the Metrovicks were rostered on was the Condor – an overnight freight service that ran from London to Glasgow and vice versa. The train was a container service that was introduced to try to combat the growing threat of road haulage. The service started on 16 March 1959 with D5710 and D5708 in charge. The Condor had three claims to fame: it could boast the longest non-stop run of any freight train, covering 301 miles from Hendon to Carlisle, where a change of crews took place; it had the longest run for any British Railways diesel, running 402 miles from Hendon to Gushetfaulds Goods Depot at Glasgow; and it was also the fastest freight train in the country.

Consignments could be booked as late as 2.30 p.m. by companies based in South or East London, or by 5.30 p.m. if within 10 miles of Hendon, to guarantee their load would make it onto that night's train. It was also guaranteed that the consignment would be delivered to any address in Glasgow by 10.30 a.m. the following morning. And how much did this service cost? Just £16 for a 300cu.ft container or £18 for a larger 700cu.ft version, which included picking up and delivering by road.

D5711 at Barrow (12E). (Keith Long)

D5714 at Carlisle on 11 July 1964. (Keith Long)

By August, trade was not sufficient enough to warrant keeping the twenty-seven long-wheelbase 'Platefit' wagons hauled by two locos and the load was cut to just thirteen wagons with one Metrovick in charge.

The locos were never free from reliability problems and they were all withdrawn in 1968. D5705 escaped the scrapyard and went into departmental use; renumbered S15705 and used by the research department on test trains. It was then relegated to heating carriages, renumbered TDB968006. Thankfully it made it into preservation and has been fully restored.

D5711 arrives at Barrow-in-Furness with a train from Preston.

A forlorn D5704 awaits the cutter's torch at Barrow Shed on 25 June 1965.

CLASS 30/31

Class 31 was one of the first classes of main-line diesel to be introduced by British Railways, appearing for the first time in November 1957. The locos were made by Brush and were diesel-electrics with a wheel arrangement of A1A-A1A, which meant they had six axles, with the middle axle on each bogie unpowered. There were 263 in the class being originally numbered D5500–D5699 and D5800-D5862.

The first thirty-five of the class were limited to a speed of 80mph, but later models were capable of 90mph. The original engines were supplied by Mirlees with Brush electrics, but these did not prove to be too successful and from 1964 they were refitted with a de-rated version of the English Electric engine fitted to the Class 37s. The engines had to be de-rated, as the Brush electrics could not cope with any more power.

D5500 at Liverpool Street on 19 March 1958. Note the lack of headcode box.

Locomotives with the original engines were Class 30s but none survived in this form to bear the number. After receiving new engines they were reclassified as Class 31s. The first examples were assigned to the Eastern Region, pulling passenger services out of Liverpool Street and performing other duties, but as more of the class were introduced they could be spotted on the Western and London Midland Regions.

Under the TOPS numbering scheme they were classified as Class 31 (originally Class 30) and were numbered 31001–31970, within which there were subclasses – e.g. they were all originally equipped for steam heating, but some were altered to electric heating and these were designated as 31/4. The first twenty locomotives had Electro-Magnetic Multiple Working control equipment and were classified as Class 31/0. These were easily recognisable as they were not fitted with headcode boxes over the cabs. As they were non-standard they were withdrawn in the late 1970s. The majority of the class was designated Class 31/1.

D5849 (31 315) on a freight train at Newark on 3 October 1964.

31 411 passes through York Station with a Scarborough–Leeds service on 27 August 1982.

31 278 at Tyne Yard, having arrived from Hexham on 7 September 1988. Note the larger number on the side of the loco.

31 430 at Edale with a Liverpool–Sheffield passenger service on 3 May 1988. The class number had been painted on the front of this loco.

A few of the class were named and this is 31 428 *North Yorkshire Moors Railway* at Hartlepool on the 5.10 p.m. Newcastle–Middlesbrough service on 7 September 1988.

31 428 and 31 461 double-head the 7.50 a.m. Great Yarmouth–Liverpool service at Whittlesey on 30 May 1987.

31 160 and 31 319 at Sutton Bridge Junction with the 10.15 a.m. Aberystwyth–Euston service on 15 August 1987.

31 445 at Boston on a Skegness–Leeds passenger service on 13 June 1987.

31 427 at Middlewich on the 10.00 a.m. Euston–Preston service on Sunday 14 February 1988.

31 407 and 31 451 head Class 87 87 005 *City of London* at Whiteacre Junction between Birmingham and Derby on 12 April 1987.

31 181, in Freight Grey livery, hauls a passenger train through Swineshead on 8 August 1987.

08 650, in Rail Blue livery but with a Railfreight sign attached, pulls a three-car DMU through Eastleigh on 14 May 1988.

D1001 *Western Pathfinder* stands outside Swindon Works on 5 July 1963. (G. Wareham)

Warship D859 *Vanquisher* stands beside Hymek D7036 alongside the turntable at Old oak Common in September 1969. (G. Wareham)

Deltic D9017 *The Durham Light Infantry* in original green livery. (G. Wareham)

Class 47 1766 having lost its 'D' prefix waits to leave Kings Cross in March 1970. Note the shed code 41A Tinsley (Sheffield) next to its number. (G. Wareham)

33 119 passes through Salisbury with a rake of Railfreight wagons on 16 July 1986.

At Derby: Not much attention appears to have been lavished on 31 461 when it took charge of the Jolly Fisherman excursion to Skegness on 9 April 1985.

20 008 and 20137 double-head a freight through South Bank Middlesbrough on 8 September 1988.

40 004 stands outside the shed at Motherwell MPD on 13 July 1984.

45 135, formerly D99 *3rd Carabinier* heads a passenger train through Derby on 13 September 1986. The loco is now preserved on the East Lancs Railway.

37 417 *Highland Region* waits to leave the Kyle of Lochalsh on 13 July 1988.

50 034 *Furious* leaves Paddington in March 1987.

47 702 *St Cuthbert* in ScotRail livery at Sighthill on 19 August 1987.

25 037 in *Reddish MPD* in February 1983. The workshops, which were built in 1954 to service the 1500v DC EM1 and EM2 overhead electric locomotives, closed a month after this photograph was taken.

26 037 in the sidings at Millerhill, Edinburgh on 10 July 1984.

31 235 in Railfreight livery at Crewe on 26 May 1990.

Only twenty-five years after railway scrapyards were full of steam locomotives, the diesels built to replace them were suffering a similar fate. This was the scene at Vic Berry's scrapyard in Leicester in May 1990.

37 009 *Typhoon* still with centre doors and headcodes on either side was spotted at Stratford on 28 April 1990.

Warship D864 *Zambesi* at Newton Abbott in May 1967. It has obviously just had a new coat of Rail Blue paint but for some reason the underframes had been left in the original maroon livery. (G. Wareham)

31 309 Cricklewood with white stripe along its body passes through Sheffield on 8 August 1987.

31 285 heads 31 286 on a freight through South Bank on 8 September 1988.

CLASS 33

Way out of their normal stomping grounds: D6570/D6578 (33052/33059) at Newark in 1962.

This class looked remarkably like the Class 26s and 27s; unsurprisingly, they were built by the same company, the BRC&W Co., but were destined for the Southern Region, rather than north of the border. Cosmetically the main difference was that the central cab window was enlarged to the same height as those either side to aid visibility. They were more powerful Type-3s, rather than Type-2s, having 1,550bhp engines supplied by Sulzer and transmissions by Crompton-Parkinson, which led to their nickname of 'Cromptons'. They were delivered in 1960 and were the only main-line diesel to be built for the Southern Region, where they became a common sight throughout. Ninety-eight examples were built (D6500–D6597). The final twelve were built to a smaller loading gauge so they could work through the tunnels between Tonbridge and Hastings.

The contractors, who built this section of track skimped on costs and lined the tunnels using less than the standard six layers of bricks stipulated. The problem came to light when Mountfield Tunnel collapsed. Inspection of the tunnels revealed that Grove Hill Tunnel had been built using only one layer of bricks. Other tunnels had been built using four layers, but this was not really sufficient. The South Eastern Railway decided that the most cost efficient way of solving the problem was to add further layers of brickwork rather than make the tunnel bore larger. This of course restricted the width of rolling stock that could be used. The loading-gauge problem was solved when the line was electrified in 1986 by singling the lines through all the tunnels.

The 33s were built with electric train heaters and before newer rolling stock came on line, they could be seen coupled to Class 24s, whose sole job was to supply heating for the passengers. D6502 was involved in a terrible collision in 1964 when it ran through red signals at Itchingfield Junction, West Sussex, ploughed into the back of a freight train and overturned, and killing the two crew members. The damage was so bad it had to be cut up on site.

On the introduction of the TOPS numbering system they were classified as Type-33s. Most were 33/0 but some became 33/1. They were equipped for push–pull working.

33 019 heads a passenger train through Westbury on 1 July 1982.

Although much of the region was electrified, in 1966 it was envisaged that it would not be economical to electrify the line between Bournemouth and Weymouth. Instead the EMUs that arrived at Bournemouth from Waterloo would be taken to and from Weymouth by Class 33s. To save running round at Weymouth, the 33s were equipped so they could propel their coaches from the rear. Nineteen of the class were converted at Eastleigh.

For use over the tramway section through the streets of Weymouth to the quay, an orange flashing light and bell had to be fitted to the front of the train and a guard walked in front to clear pedestrians and badly parked cars.

The Hastings gauge locos were classified as 33/2s. Having to fit all the equipment into these narrower bodies proved very expensive to the BRC&W Co. and was one of the factors that led to its downfall. They were known locally as 'Slim Jims'.

Although there is relatively little industry within the Southern Region, freight workings were not unknown and the 33s could be seen hauling aggregate loads from Cliffe and cement trains from Northfleet. They were in charge of Speedlink services to Dover Docks, where they could also be seen on shunting duties. They had relatively long lives, surviving into a time when the preservation of diesels was becoming popular, which is why twenty-six examples have been preserved.

33 108 coupled to an electric unit at Salisbury on 16 July 1986.

33 015 and 33 118 head a freight train through Reading on 21 August 1982.

D6516 pulls a 4TC through Micheldever in 1967 (G. Wareham)

CLASS 35

D7027 in original livery at Bristol Bath Road on 3 August 1963.

These locomotives were commonly known as Hymeks due to their Mekydro design hydraulic transmission. There were 101 in the class and they were all introduced to the Western Region from 1961–64. Designed as medium-powered locos for use on secondary passenger and freight duties, they were built by Beyer Peacock at Gorton, Manchester. Beyer Peacock wanted a larger share of the diesel production and put forward the design for a Type-3 locomotive (1501–1750hp). Type-2s (D63xx) and Type-4s (Warships) were being built but there had been no plans for a Type-3 medium-powered loco. A consortium was formed between Beyer Peacock and Bristol-Siddeley to build locomotives powered by Bristol-Siddeley/Maybach engines coupled to Stone-Maybach hydraulic gearboxes.

The BTC placed an order for forty-five locos, but, before the first one was introduced, a further order for fifty and a final order for six were placed. The first example was handed over to the Western Region at Paddington Station on 16 May 1961. At the time they were the most powerful single-engine diesel hydraulic, with a maximum speed of 90mph. The livery was more detailed than the Warships that had been delivered earlier. Although the main body was painted Brunswick green it was detailed with a lime-green stripe along the bottom and the cab windows were picked out in white giving them a very striking appearance. Yellow warning panels were added later. When Rail Blue was adopted it was applied all over at first, but the white cab surrounds were soon reinstated. The final livery was blue with full yellow ends and cab surrounds. Many of the class did not get repainted into blue and were withdrawn in the original green livery, albeit some with full yellow ends. The fleet numbers were made from cast aluminium rather than painted on as in other classes.

D7063 passing Southall on 22 July 1964.

D7065 at Southall on 22 July 1964.

Although they were designed for hauling secondary passenger services, some were used on Paddington–Cardiff–Swansea express services before they were later replaced by the Western Class. Apart from tracks west of Plymouth, they were a common sight all over the region and were often seen on regional freight services. They were all withdrawn in the early 1970s as British Railways wished to standardise their diesel-electrics and were replaced by Class 37s that had been displaced from other areas due to falling traffic demands. None survived long enough to receive a Class 35 TOPS number. Four have survived into preservation.

D7047 on the sea wall at Teignmouth on 18 August 1963.

D7011 in original green livery at Bristol Bath Road (82A) in April 1966.

Awaiting the cutter's torch: D7046 in August 1971.

CLASS 37

Class 37s were categorised as Type-3 (1,500–1999bhp) because of their power output of 1,750bhp and were built by English Electric at their works in the Vulcan Foundry at Newton-Le-Willows and by Robert Stephenson and Hawthorns at Darlington. They were successful in their bid to construct these Type-3s as they had already introduced reliable Type-1s and Type-4s. They had also exported some Type-3s to Africa and used these a basis for the design of the 37s. They bore more than a passing resemblance to their previous designs – Class 40s and Baby Deltics, Class 23s.

6701 in original green livery having lost its 'D' prefix but gained full yellow ends. At Saltley in November 1969. (G. Wareham)

The first order was for forty-two examples. Introduced in late 1960, these were numbered D6700–D6741. More orders followed and the whole class was numbered D6700–D6999 and D6600–D6608, making a total of 309. Under the TOPS scheme they became 37 001–37 308, with D6701 becoming 37 001 and the rest following in sequence. The only difference was that D6700 was renumbered 37 119. This was because D6719 had been written off in an accident with D1671 following a landslip in South Wales. D6600–D6608 became 37 300–37 308. The first ones to be introduced were allocated to the Eastern Region and hauled express services out of Liverpool Street. They became a common sight over most of the network and, with a light axle loading, they were allowed over many lines that had weight restrictions where other main-line locos were not permitted.

It took five years for the entire class to come on stream, with the last batch being allocated to the Western Region. The class was subject to many alterations over its lifetime, and under the TOPS scheme, these variations became subsections of the class: 37/0 meant that no alteration had been

37 031 (D6731) at Melton Ross on an Immingham–Doncaster train of empties on 28 October 1987.

made, 37/3 meant that they had been re-bogied, and 37/4 meant they were converted from steam heating to electric train heating. The latter were used on passenger services in Scotland and Wales.

A number of locos were assigned to freight-only duties. These were 37/5s and 37/7s – the difference between the two being that the 37/7s were given added ballast to cope with the heavier metal and coal freights in South Wales. In the late 1980s some were fitted with Mirrles and Ruston engines. These were intended for use in the new Class 38 freight loco. The converted 37s became 37/9s and were to be seen as a test bed. Although they were successful, the 38s never materialised.

As in other classes, some locos were given split headcode indicators on either side of the nose to give access between locos through centrally placed doors. When these were phased out, centrally placed headcodes were introduced.

The early locos were delivered in British Railways green livery with a grey roof. A small yellow warning panel was added to later deliveries, and by the late 1960s this warning panel had been enlarged to cover the entire nose.

37 062 (D6762) at Boston on 1 June 1988. It was in charge of a Sheffield–Skegness passenger service. The original indicator boxes are no longer used and lights have been fitted in their place.

37 424 (D6979, 37 279) *Glendarroch* on the 12.30 p.m. Mallaig–Fort William service. Note the centrally placed route indicator box, again redundant and being used for lights. The Highland terrier logo denotes it was shedded at Eastfield.

37 510 (D6812 37 112) at Hartlepool on 5 September 1988 en route for Ferryhill.

37 798 (D6706 37 006) in Freight Grey livery with a train of coal hoppers bound for Aberthaw power station on 9 March 1987.

Rail Blue was introduced soon after complete with yellow nose. Another change occurred in the late 1970s when the large double arrow logo was introduced together with the yellow wrapped around to cover the whole nose. The tops of the noses were painted matt black to reduce glare. Locomotives destined for freight work were painted in Freight Grey.

In 1987, subsectors were introduced and a three-tone grey colour scheme was applied to coal, metals, petroleum, distribution and construction locos. Each sector also had a logo that was added to the grey livery. After the break-up of British Rail, more liveries started to appear. Loadhaul locos were adorned with an orange and black livery, Main Line locos were painted in blue with a silver stripe, English, Welsh & Scottish Railways (EWS) were maroon, while departmental locomotives sported a grey and yellow livery. Individual depots started adding logos to their allocation. Inverness locos were given stags, Eastfield were given Highland terriers and Canton Cardiff liveries were adorned with Celtic dragons.

Some 37s were exported to other countries when there was no more work in this country. Some could be seen in France and Spain helping with their construction of high-speed railways. Their long lives and route availability have led to them being popular with preservationists and, as a result, forty-eight locomotives have been saved from the cutter's torch.

37 408 (D6989 37 289) Loch Rannoch, Fort William, heading for Mallaig on 6 July 1988.

37 175 (D6875) on a Fort William–Glasgow service on 20 July 1985.

37 183 (D6883) on shed at Polmadie (66A) on 20 July 1985.

37 419 (D6991 37 291) in InterCity livery at Southport waiting to depart for Manchester Victoria on 27 April 1992.

CLASS 40

There were 200 Class 40s introduced between 1958–1962. The initial order was one for ten locomotives, D200–D209. Their pedigree can be traced back to the Southern Region's 10203, with the first ten using an English Electric engine, identical bogies and drive train. When first introduced they were very well thought of and used on express passenger services out of Liverpool Street to Norwich and on the East Coast Main Line (ECML). They could only produce 2,000bhp and their performances were not deemed to be a marked improvement on the *Britannia* and other 4-6-2 Pacific steam locomotives, which they had been designed to replace. The Eastern Region declined any further Class 40s, preferring to carry on with steam until the Class 55 Deltics were ready.

D207 (40 007) at Newark on 14 July 1967.

40 151 at Manchester Victoria on 19 July 1978. This was one of the locos made with old-style headcode discs.

Still at Manchester Victoria and 40 144, one of the twenty examples with side-mounted destination panels, trundles through on a freight run.

D326, another example of the side-mounted destination panels waits at Willesden in August 1967. (G. Wareham)

They did find a home on the ECML for a short period. They were capable of hauling expresses up Camden Bank and the lack of investment on the West Coast Main Line (WCML) meant that the average speeds were lower than on the ECML and their duties proved to be within their capabilities. They were displaced from these routes on the completion of the overhead electrification. Despite this mixed reception, a further 190 were ordered. Twenty (D305–D324) of these were built by Robert Stephenson and Hawthorns, the rest produced by English Electric. They were all delivered in British Railways green livery, but there were some design differences. The earlier examples (D200–D324) had disc headcodes, but the design was altered to cater for British Railways' new four-character train numbers. The twenty locos built by Stephenson and Hawthorns had split boxes on either side of the central end doors. When it was decided to discontinue use of these doors, the design was altered and displays were moved to the centre of the engine.

Their position as pride of the fleet did not last for long, however, as more powerful locomotives, Class 47s, were introduced before the final Class 40s could be delivered. Their duties on top-link passenger work were soon put in the hands of these more powerful engines and the Class 40s were soon to be seen on secondary passenger and freight work. D326 gained infamy as it was hauling the train involved in the Great Train Robbery in 1963.

When the TOPS numbering scheme was introduced, they were renumbered 40 001–40 199 and given a coat of Rail Blue at about the same time. D210–D235 were given names of ocean liners owned by Cunard, Elder Dempster Lines and Canadian Pacific Steamships. This is because they were based in the Liverpool area and ran services to and from these companies' home port. The nameplates were removed when the locos were moved away from the area.

As they got older, they were seen less and less in the southern half of the country. They were only fitted with steam-heating capabilities. As newer coaching stock equipped with electric heating came online they were relegated to heavy freight workings. Their last regular passenger duties were in Scotland and on the North Wales Coast Line to Holyhead. This was in 1980. They were pressed into service on weekend excursions and filling in for electric locos on the WCML when the need arose. Gradual withdrawal of the class started

40 060 at Newton Heath on 4 April 1983. This is one of the batch that was equipped with a centrally located destination panel.

in 1976, but it was not until the 1980s before they started disappearing in greater numbers. The last of the class to be given an overhaul was 40 167, at Crewe Works in February 1981.They may not have been one of the operators' favourite engines but they did have a large following of enthusiasts.

By the end of 1984, only sixteen examples remained. This included 40 122, which was the original D200. It had been assigned this number as D322 had been scrapped in 1967 due to severe accident damage. It had been withdrawn in 1981, but reinstated in July 1983. This came about because two enthusiasts noticed it languishing on a scrap line at Carlisle Kingmoor awaiting being moved to Swindon to be cut up. Apart from this engine, the last of the class was withdrawn in early 1985. They persuaded British Railways not to scrap it and it was taken to Toton for complete overhaul, which included a repaint into its original green livery. It was then used to haul enthusiasts' specials. Four locomotives were transferred to departmental use as Class 97s and these were used in the remodelling of Crewe Station before withdrawal in 1987. 40 122 was finally withdrawn in 1988 and presented to the National Railway Museum. Six other examples have been preserved.

CLASS 41

D600 *Active* ready to leave Plymouth North with the *Cornish Riviera Express* on 4 June 1962. (Charles Verrall)

D600–D604 were five Warship Class diesel-hydraulic locomotives built for the Western Region. They were introduced in 1958–59 and were classified as Class 41 under the TOPS system, but none lasted long enough to receive a number under that system. They differed from the Class 42 and 43 Warships in that they were much heavier (117 tons) and needed six axles in a A1A-A1A formation as against the four axles B-B of the lighter examples (78 tons). The Western Region never wanted these locomotives but the BTC wanted a diesel hydraulic as a direct comparison with the Class 40s that were entering production. The D600 class relied on two large slow revving engines to produce its power whereas the D800 types used two smaller high-revving engines. Unusually they had spoked wheels. They were able to be coupled either together or with one of the D63xx diesels. They were all named after British Warships.

They began trials in Scotland near to the manufacturer's North British headquarters in Glasgow, before being assigned to Swindon. D600 Active was at the head of a run put on for the press when it ran from Paddington to Bristol and back on 17 February 1958. The twin engines came in handy when one engine failed on the return journey, and it finished the trip using the one remaining engine.

D602 *Bulldog* at Plymouth in July 1966, sporting Rail Blue livery and still with side-indicator boxes and central doors. (G. Wareham)

The whole of the class was eventually all assigned to Laira where they were put in charge of Paddington–Penzance expresses. D601 was the first diesel to be in charge of the Cornish Riviera Express on 16 May 1958. They were all introduced in the standard British Railways green livery of the time. D602 was repainted in Rail Blue with small yellow panels and D600 ended its days in Rail Blue with full yellow ends. They were able to run at speeds of 90mph and were even clocked at 100mph.

They were all withdrawn in December 1967. This was not because they were unreliable, but because British Railways had decreed that the number of main-line diesel classes had to be reduced from tweny-eight to fifteen by 1974. D600 and D601 lingered at Woodhams scrapyard at Barry, whereas the other three were sent to Cashmores of Newport, where the end came much quicker. None of the class survives – indeed, no diesel made by North British has been preserved.

CLASS 42 and 43

D800, with disc rather than blind headcodes, heads over Cowley Bridge Junction. The nameplate reads: 'The first 2000bhp diesel hydraulic locomotive for British Railways'.

D808 *Centaur* on the Cornish Riviera Express at Paddington in 1960.

The Warships, as they were commonly known, were introduced between 1958 and 1961. At the time, the German railways were more advanced in the introduction of diesel locomotives so the Western Region turned to them for guidance. Their V200 was proving to be successful, but was too big for the British loading gauge, so they could not be purchased off the shelf. Instead a licence was obtained to build smaller versions within the UK.

Initially there was an order to build three (D800–D802). These were slightly underpowered compared to the rest as the gearboxes could not handle any more than the 1035bhp they generated, but later improvements to the gearbox made it possible for the power to be increased to 1135bhp, so engines were upgraded accordingly. These first three also had minor cosmetic differences including still using discs rather than blinds for headcodes.

In all, seventy-one of the class were built including thirty-eight built at British Railways' own works at Swindon (D800–D832 and D866–D870) while another thirty-three were built by the North British Locomotive Company (D834–D865).

Double-headed D818 *Glory* and D828 *Magnificent* turn heads as they pass along the sea wall at Teignmouth on 8 August 1963.

North British Warship D845 *Sprightly* leaving Bristol Temple Meads on 3 August 1963.

The latter locos were classified as Class 43s rather than the Class 42s built by British Railways, although none survived long enough to receive a TOPS number. The engines for the Class 42s were Maybachs made under licence by Bristol Siddeley at Filton, Bristol, with the gearboxes being supplied by Mekydro. The 43s were fitted with MAN engines coupled to Voith gearboxes. They were relatively lightweight being less than 80 tons as compared to a Class 40 that weighed about 140 tons. This helped when climbing the gradients between Exeter and Plymouth. Like their German relatives, they were powered by diesel hydraulics rather than diesel electrics being pioneered on other parts of the network. D830 *Majestic* was fitted with two British-designed Paxman Ventura engines so comparisons could be made between the two.

They were allocated to Old Oak Common (81A), Bristol Bath Road (82A) Laira Plymouth (84A) and Newton Abbott (83A) where they were put in charge of the express trains from Paddington to the South West, displacing the Kings and Castles. In October 1958, D800 became the first of the class to head the Cornish Riviera Express from Penzance to Paddington. Despite being

Another shot of Teignmouth, this time with D849 *Superb* in charge of a passenger train.

officially restricted to 90mph, the class on several occasions achieved speeds of over 100mph. As the more powerful Western Class were introduced, they displaced some of the Warship duties, but they found more work hauling services from Waterloo to destinations in the west of the Southern Region.

Apart from D800, which was named after the chairman of the BTC, Sir Brian Robertson, and D812 *The Royal Naval Reserve*, the class were named after British warships. This was done in alphabetical order, which caused a problem when five more were unexpectedly ordered from British Railways and some juggling of names was required within the batch being ordered from North British.

All the Warships were delivered in an all-over green livery, but during the 1960s the management of the Western Region decided that their main-line locomotives should be painted maroon and some of the class were so painted. By the end of the decade Rail Blue was being standardised on all of British Railways' fleet and D864 *Zambesi* was the first to bear this livery. The last of the class to lose its green livery was D810 *Cockade* in 1970. Yellow panels and then full yellow ends were adopted on all of the class. Some kept their maroon livery until they were withdrawn. From 1968, following the end of steam, they lost the prefix D when they went in for repaints.

In the late 1960s, the Warships were used to double-head the Cornish Riviera when the 222-mile run was retimed to three hours forty-five minutes. Not all the locomotives in the class were modified to allow both engines to be driven by one driver, but the tight schedule did put a strain on the engines. The first three years in the operation of these diesel hydraulics had been relatively trouble-free, but problems started to develop in 1961–62. Their German counterparts also started having similar problems at the same time even though theirs were three years older. On one day in November 1962 almost a third of the Western Region's main-line locomotives were not serviceable, with many of them sidelined with transmission problems. In 1967, the hierarchy in British Railways decreed that the all diesel hydraulics should be replaced as soon as possible by diesel electrics, thus spelling the end for the Warships.

It was not only their unreliability that counted against them. It had been envisaged in the 1955 Modernisation Plan that all goods wagons would have brakes fitted, but this had not happened, so goods trains had to rely on the locomotive brakes and it was decided that locomotives with only four axles would not have enough stopping power. It had also been impossible to convert them to electric train heating. Civil engineering restrictions were relaxed at about the same time so that Co-Co diesel electrics of greater power were now allowed over the tracks. Advances in electric traction also brought down the weight of electric traction motors quite considerably so the overall weight of a typical Co-Co locomotive came down from 135 tons to 115 tons. This meant that the power/weight advantage that diesel hydraulics had once enjoyed had been gradually whittled away. Diesel electrics had become cheaper to produce, and combined with the fact that the distance between engine top overhauls had been extended to 16,000 hours and 300–400 per cent superiority in oil consumption had been achieved; the writing was on the wall for diesel hydraulics. The class had disappeared from the network by the end of 1972.

D821 *Greyhound* became the first main-line diesel to be preserved. This came about because a group had approached British Railways with a view to buying Class 22 D6319. A price had been agreed, but it was scrapped at Swindon before the new owners could collect it, so a choice of Warships was offered in its place. As well as D821, D832 *Onslaught* has also been preserved.

D846 *Steadfast* passing Laira Junction signal box with the 10.30 a.m. Plymouth–Paddington service, 4 June 1962. (Charles Verrall)

D862 *Viking* passing Old Oak Common on 19 August 1962. (Charles Verrall)

D804 *Avenger* at Paddington in 1960.

CLASSES 44, 45 and 46 'PEAKS'

D2 (44 0020) *Helvellyn* at its home shed of Toton on 7 September 1971.

Classes 44, 45 and 46 were almost identical but were introduced at different stages. There were only ten Class 44s ordered (D1–D10; 44 001–44 010) and they were all named after mountains in the UK, hence their nickname 'Peaks'. They were Type-4 diesels powered by Sulzer engines coupled to six Crompton Parkinson nose-suspended traction motors. They were introduced in 1959–60, having been built at the British Railways works in Derby. A further 127 locomotives were ordered (D11–D138) with an increase of 200bhp.

These were classified as Class 45s (45 001–45 077 and 45 101–45 150) and introduced in 1960–62. Crewe Works was also awarded the construction of this batch, which they shared with Derby. Some of these subsequently received names mainly of British Army regiments.

The final order that was allotted to Derby was for fifty-five locomotives (D138–D193) and these were introduced between 1961–63. They were classified as Class 46s (46 001–46 056) and differed from the Class 45s in that their traction motors were supplied by Brush rather than Crompton Parkinson. They were all of 1Co-Co1, which meant that the axle at either end was not driven as the other six were. They were all built with steam-heating capabilities but with the introduction of newer rolling stock that used electric heating, fifty were converted and these were reclassified as 45/1s. The Class 44s were fitted with headcode discs and end doors to allow crews to access cabs on the move. The Class 45s were equipped with indicator panels with the first of the class having them on the front edges. Although the doors were rarely used, as very few workings required double-heading, they were

D14 (45 015), with headcodes on the sides rather than in the centre, pictured at Nottingham.

D108 (45 012) at Nottingham in 1961 showing the split headcode on the front.

D174 (46 037) at Newark on 15 June 1963.

D21 (45 026), home shed 41A Tinsley (Sheffield) at Gloucester on 30 May 1966.

retained until when, on later examples to be built, the headcode was moved to a central position. They were split into two parts so doors could still be used. When the practice of using headcodes was abandoned, the headcode panels were covered over.

The Class 44s were initially used on passenger services between the capital and the north, but when the Class 45s became available the steam-heating boilers were removed and they were assigned purely to freight workings and were allotted to Toton Shed (16A). From there, they hauled coal trains in the Derbyshire and Nottinghamshire areas.

The Class 45s handled most of the passenger traffic out of St Pancras to the Midlands until 1982 when they were gradually ousted by the arrival of the High-Speed Trains (HST). They could also be spotted further north operating over the Pennines from Liverpool to York, Newcastle and Scarborough.

The Class 46s were regularly seen on freight and passenger services between the North East and the South West, including hauling china clay trains from Cornwall to the Potteries. Gateshead (52A), Cardiff (86A) and Plymouth (84A) were all originally allotted some, but towards the end of their working lives, they were all shedded at Gateshead.

D176 (46039) at Claypole on 28 May 1963.

45 050 at Birmingham New Street on a Paignton–Liverpool passenger service on 2 May 1984.

In July 1984, 46 009 (D146) was deliberately destroyed when it was used to demonstrate the safety of the nuclear flasks that were being used to transfer nuclear waste on the railways. A flask was placed across the tracks and the locomotive with four Mk1 coaches rammed it. The test took place at the Old Dalby Test Track. An extra brake cock was installed on the sole bar. The driver opened the throttle before jumping from the cab and releasing the brakes. The invited guests, who were sitting in specially erected grandstands, must have breathed a collective sigh of relief when the dust settled and it became clear that the flask had survived intact.

Withdrawal of the Class 45s started in the early 1980s, and by the end of the decade they had all disappeared from the network. Although slightly newer, no Class 46s were converted to electric heating and the withdrawal of the class started earlier, in 1977, with the last one disappearing in 1984. In all, sixteen examples have been preserved.

45 059 *Royal Engineer* on the 09.36 a.m. Leeds–Plymouth relief at Exeter on 21 April 1984.

CLASS 47

There were 512 Class 47s built, making them the most numerous class of diesel on British Railways. Their existence came about because of a need for a powerful Type-4 diesel-electric locomotive that weighed less than the Class 40s, 44s and 45s already introduced. The 1Co-Co1-wheel arrangement on these locos, designed to spread the weight over eight axles and thereby save wear on rails, had not been successful and was possibly proving to be detrimental. Instead, a Co-Co design was required.

The 47s were powered by Sulzer twelve-cylinder engines, initially producing 2,750bhp. They were soon derated to 2,580bhp to aid reliability. The initial order was for twenty (D1500–D1519), which were built before two experimental locomotives, D0260 *Lion* and D0280 *Falcon*, could be

D1556 at Liverpool Street on 23 October 1965.

properly assessed. A large number of Type-4 diesels were needed to replace the number of steam engines that were rapidly being phased out. A second order for 270 was placed with further orders making a total of 512. The majority, 310, were constructed at the Brush Works in Loughborough and the remaining 202 at British Railways' works at Derby. These were numbered D1500–D1999 and D1100–D1111.

Five locomotives (D1702-D1706) were fitted with a different twelve-cylinder Sulzer engine and classified as Class 48s, but these were not successful and were converted to Class 47s. D1500, the first of the class, was introduced in 1962, making its revenue-earning debut pulling a return passenger service between Kings Cross and Hull on 8 October 1962. In their time, the class could be seen hauling both passenger and freight services over the entire network.

Of this class, eighty-one were designed for freight duties only and were not fitted with any train heating capabilities. The others were initially equipped for steam heating, and later models had electric heating capabilities to cope with the newer rolling stock being introduced.

D1551 on a passenger train at Newark, 17 July 1965.

In the early 1970s, when the TOPs numbering system was introduced, they were renumbered 47xxx and subdivided into different classes. 47/0 meant they were unaltered with steam heating, 47/3 meant they were the freight only locos with no heating and 47/4 specified that they were equipped with electric heating. 47 046 had been damaged in an accident near Peterborough and was chosen as a test bed for a new sixteen-cylinder Ruston engine that was to be used in the Class 56s. It was then renumbered 47 601. In 1979 it was re-engined again, this time with a twelve-cylinder Ruston engine that was to be used in the Class 58s, and was renumbered yet again to 47 901. It kept this engine until it was withdrawn in 1990.

There was another subclass – 47/7. These were push-pull fitted and designed to replace the ageing Class 27s that were being used in pairs on the Glasgow–Edinburgh shuttle service. They were also fitted with larger fuel tanks and allowed to run at 100mph. Later, they also took over the Glasgow–Aberdeen service. As a result, a further four locos had to be converted, making a total of sixteen. 47 798 was named *Prince William* and 47 799 *Prince Henry*, both of which were used on royal trains. A number of locos were given

D1514 pulling a trial train of roadrailers through Newark Northgate on 25 April 1963.

47/8 numbers and these were 47/4s equipped with larger fuel tanks. After privatisation, Virgin Trains used these on their cross-country routes, but they were gradually displaced by the new Voyager trains.

The class were delivered in two-tone green livery and yellow front panels were soon added. Like other classes they were gradually painted in Rail Blue with full yellow ends. Many lasted well into privatisation and they could be seen in a variety of liveries including ScotRail, Anglia, Railfreight, InterCity, Advenza and ECML.

By 1986, only five of the class had been withdrawn and these were due to accident damage. The next to go were the original twenty, by then numbered 47 401–47 420. However, it took six years to withdraw these, with the first going in 1988 and the last in 1992. Some locos with non-standard electrical equipment were the next to be targeted, but a surplus of spare parts meant that the rate of withdrawal was slow, with only sixty-one locos scrapped

47 450 *Aycliffe* at Wolverhampton on 6 April 1990.

47 576 *Kings Lynn*, sporting Network South East livery, at Ely on 19 June 1987.

before the start of 1993. Privatisation saw the need for more engines, and the new companies used the 47s until more modern locomotives could be delivered. Fewer than 100 examples disappeared between 1996 and 2006.

The increase in the use of electric multiple units meant the end for a few more examples. Despite this, by the end of 2014, there were still twenty-nine locomotives in active service being run by companies that included Direct Rail Services, the charter companies West Coast Railway Company and Riviera Trains. Others are being used by Colas for track maintenance work.

Thirty-three locomotives were equipped with EMD engines and reclassified as Class 57s and are in use by private companies. Apart from these, over thirty have been preserved.

47 484 *Isambard Kingdom Brunel*, in green livery, spotted at Old Oak Common on 28 April 1990.

47 471 *Norman Tunna GC*, in InterCity livery, passing through Eastleigh on 14 May 1988.

47 589, in another version of InterCity livery, heads 87 034 through Castle Bromwich on 27 March 1989.

47 333 *Civil Link*, in grey livery at Bescot open day on 6 May 1990.

47 372 crossing High Street Lincoln on 17 March 1984.

47 078 at Cardiff Central on 22 February 1984.

CLASS 50

The Class 50 diesel locomotives were built following successful trials of DP2. Although it resembled a Deltic, many of its systems, including electronic controls were used in the Class 50s. In 1966 there was a need for fifty powerful diesel locomotives to take over expresses on the WCML to work the trains north from Crewe to Scotland where overhead electrification had not reached. They were often used double-headed, so they could match the 100mph speeds of the electrics they replaced.

British Railways were not prepared to buy any locomotives for what they envisaged would be for a limited period, so they leased them from

D415 (50 015) at Glasgow Polmadie on 6 April 1969.

50 003 *Temeraire* at Doncaster Works on 4 July 1979.

English Electric. They were built at the Vulcan Foundry at Newton-le-Willows between the start of 1967 and the end of 1968. They were numbered D400–D449. After the end of steam on the network the prefix 'D' was dropped and they became 400–449, and in the mid 1970s under the TOPS scheme they became 50 001–50 050, with D400 becoming 50 050 and the others keeping their last two digits. After electrification was completed, they were transferred to the Western Region, where they took over the duties operated by the ageing Western Class. British Railways bought the locos as they were transferred.

Originally they had not been named, but the Western Region wanted to keep their tradition of naming their express engines and they named them all after Royal Navy warships. 50 035 was the first to be named, becoming *Ark Royal*. When the HSTs were introduced they could still be seen in the West Country but were in charge of services out of Waterloo. They were also put in charge of services from the capital to Birmingham and Bristol. With reliability proving to be a problem in the 1980s, a lot of the complex electrics were disposed of during major refurbishments.

They were all initially delivered in Rail Blue livery with yellow fronts. During refurbishments, the route indicator panels were removed and headlights fitted in their place. The livery was also changed to include wrap-around yellow ends. 50 023 *Howe* was the first to appear in this livery. A much larger British Railways logo was added, totally transforming their appearance. 50 014 *Warspite* was the last of the class to receive such treatment. 50 007 *Hercules* was repainted into Bruswick green and renamed *Sir Edward Elgar* to commemorate the 150th anniversary of the GWR. The depot at Laira also gave 50 019 *Ramilles* a coat of a variation of Rail Blue.

In 1986, Network South East took over the services being operated out of Waterloo by the Class 50s and some of the locos were repainted in this garish livery, which had two variations; one having a white cab surround, the other blue. The upswept red and white stripes also disappeared and the blue was altered to a darker shade.

In an effort to find more work from for the class, 50 049 *Defiance* was renumbered 50 149 and given modified Class 37 lower-geared bogies. It was tried hauling china clay freight trains from Cornwall and heavy stone trains from Devon quarries. It was painted in Freight Grey livery for this work. The trial was not a success and *Defiance* was returned to its previous livery in 1989. Reliability was becoming a problem again, and Class 47s and DMUs started taking over their duties.

50 039 *Implacable* hauling an HST through Exeter on 21 April 1984.

50 046 *Ajax* at Birmingham New Street on 24 April 1984.

50 035 *Ark Royal* in Network South East (NSE) livery at Paddington on 21 March 1987.

50 002 *Superb* and 50 050 *Fearless* in the later NSE livery at Exeter on 2 June 1990.

50 015 in Dutch grey and yellow livery at Coalville on 2 May 1991.

The class was much loved by enthusiasts, and towards the end of their lives some were repainted into various liveries and used on enthusiasts' specials. 50 050 *Fearless* was painted back into its original blue livery and given its D400 identity back. 50 015 was given a coat of 'Dutch' civil engineers grey and yellow paint.

They were withdrawn between 1987 and 1994, when the last two, 50 007 and 50 050, hauled a final farewell tour on the route Waterloo–Exeter–Paddington. It was called the *50 Terminator*.

50 007 *Sir Edward Elgar*, resplendent in green livery, at Par on 22 July 1986.

CLASS 52

The Class 52s were one of the best-loved classes of diesels ever produced. They were known as 'Westerns', as the first word of their name was Western. They never survived long enough to receive a TOPS number, being the last locos to keep the old number, possibly because they bore cast-aluminium number plates rather than stick-on numbers. There were seventy-four of the class produced between 1961 and 1964 and, like other classes introduced to the Western Region of the time, they were diesel hydraulics. They were designed as it was becoming evident that a more powerful locomotive was needed than the Warship Class already in service.

D1000 *Western Enterprise* at Severn Tunnel Junction on 20 July 1964.

The Westerns had 1,350bhp and were capable of speeds up to 90mph. The advantages of diesel hydraulics over diesel electrics were that the locomotives were lighter and had a much better power-to-weight ratio and it was thought that track wear would be much less. The downside was that diesel-hydraulic transmissions could only handle 1500bhp and more powerful locomotives would need two engines and two gearboxes, as was the case with the Westerns. They were powered by two Maybach MD655 engines coupled to Voith, rather than Mekydro, transmissions.

D1000 was delivered in November 1961 sporting an all over desert sand livery. D1002–D1004 were given a coat of green paint, D1015 had a golden ochre colour scheme, while the rest of the class were delivered in maroon. The vast majority were delivered with yellow warning panels. From 1966, the Westerns started to receive the new Rail Blue livery with full yellow ends, which extended to include the cab window surrounds.

The coupling of the Maybach engine to the Voith transmission was not entirely successful and, as engines began to wear, the top speed of 90mph was increasingly difficult to achieve. When the electrification of the West Coast Line was complete the Class 50s became surplus to requirements and

D1021 *Western Cavalier* at Canton Cardiff (86A) on 29 October 1965.

D1054 *Western Governor* at Neath on 19 July 1964.

were transferred to the Western Region, where they replaced the Westerns on express services out of Paddington. Their replacement was also caused by the fact that they could not be converted to electric train heating, which the Mk2 carriages needed and the Class 47s and 50s were fitted with. They were all withdrawn between 1973 and 1977. Seven have survived into preservation.

D1071 *Western Renown* at Canton, Cardiff (86A) on 13 October 1968.

D1045 *Western Viscount* at Canton, Cardiff (86A) on 13 October 1968.

CLASS 55

Twenty-two Class 55 Deltic locomotives were built following the successful trials of the original Deltic DP1. They were built by English Electric and purchased under a service contract that meant that they would be maintained by the constructors. Further engines were purchased, so that should any major works be required a replacement could be fitted quickly while the remedial work was undertaken on the faulty engine. The engines were powerful Napier Deltics producing 1,650bhp each, and two were fitted to each loco, giving a total of 3,300bhp. These were originally marine engines with an output of 3,100bhp each but de-rated to aid longevity. (Napier was an engine manufacturer that had been bought out by English Electric.)

D9019 *Royal Highland Fusilier* heading the Flying Scotsman service near Newark on 17 July 1965.

They were all manufactured in 1961–62 and were built to work the ECML services from Kings Cross to Edinburgh with the twenty-two diesels replacing the fifty-five Gresley Pacifics. They managed this successfully, as they were able to run at 100mph and, following track improvements, managed to bring the running time of the *Flying Scotsman* down to five hours, thirty minutes including a stop at Newcastle. This beat the best time recorded by a steam engine by thirty minutes.

Delivered in a green livery with a lighter strip of green along the bottom of the bodywork, the window surrounds were painted white. Yellow warning panels were soon added to their fronts. They were all assigned to Finsbury Park (34G), Gateshead (52A) or Haymarket (64B). From 1966 they all received a coat of corporate Rail Blue. At the same time, they were converted from vacuum brakes to air brakes. In the 1970s, conversion to electric heating from steam heating was begun, in order to cope with the new rolling stock that was being introduced. In 1979 Finsbury Park Depot gave six of their engines a white surround to the cab windows, but when they were reassigned to York in their final days this was returned to blue. All were given names, but not all

D9012 *Crepello* on *The Talisman* on 13 June 1964.

from the same category. Locos shedded at Haymarket and Gateshead were named after British Army regiments, while those at Finsbury Park followed LNER practice of naming their locos after racehorses.

In 1978 InterCity HSTs, capable of 125mph, were introduced. The Deltics were kept working the same lines but placed on less glamorous work hauling parcel, newspaper and sleeper services. The entire class was withdrawn in 1980–81, apart from three examples that were kept for pulling an enthusiasts' special. This was on 2 January 1982, when 55 015 *Tulyar* left Kings Cross for Edinburgh, with 55 022 *Royal Scots Grey* on the return journey. 55 009 *Alycidon* shadowed the special all the way in case of breakdowns. These three were withdrawn at York directly after heading the special.

Six of the class were preserved and it was never envisaged that they would be allowed over British Railways metals again. On privatisation, Railtrack took over and allowed preserved locomotives access to their tracks – for a fee, of course! In 1996 the Deltic Fund became a limited company, Deltic D9000 Locomotives Ltd, with a view to running specials over the main line again. *Royal Scots Grey* was the first engine to do this and, since then,

D9000 *Royal Scots Grey* at Haymarket on 3 June 1963.

55 007 *Pinza* stands at Doncaster Works on 12 August 1979.

Having lost its 'D' prefix, 9005 *The Prince of Wales Own Regiment of Yorkshire* is seen here at Barrow Hill on 3 September 1972.

A sad sight at Doncaster Works as 55 011 *The Royal Northumberland Fusiliers* is broken up on 21 November 1982.

D9011 *The Royal Northumberland Fusiliers* in better days at Grantham, 31 May 1963.

D9016 *Gordon Highlander*, has emulated this feat. It was, for a time, painted in the purple livery of Porterbrook Leasing, which helped with its restoration.

The future is looking good for more main-line running of other preserved examples.

55 015 *Tulyar* at Doncaster Works on 17 October 1982.

EPILOGUE:
WHAT NEXT?

Why stop here? No Class 59s, 60s or 66s. Well it's probably a personal thing. The locos I have written about are classes that I can remember from my trainspotting days. They were all built in this country and not imported from America or Spain. Will the later 'foreign' locos have the same following? Will the falling number of rail enthusiasts have the same enthusiasm to preserve examples of these, which to my mind lack any character? And, of course, passenger services are now all operated by bland diesel multiple units. Who will save these for posterity? Will Joe Public in the future be flocking to a preserved railway to enjoy a ride on a Sprinter or HST unit? Will a Eurostar ever trundle through the Yorkshire countryside between Pickering and Whitby? Probably not, but who knows?

It was not long ago that the Bluebell Railway in Sussex only operated steam services and diesels were not allowed over the line, but earlier this year, when two Deltics operated services there, it was one of their busiest periods.

Perhaps you are like me and prefer looking back to the past than looking forward to the future. Writing this book has been an enjoyable nostalgic trip back into the past for me, and I hope you have enjoyed reading it as much as I have enjoyed writing it.

If you enjoyed this book, you may also be interested in…

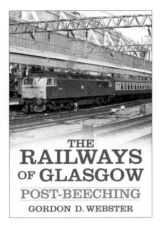

The Railways of Glasgow: Post-Beeching

GORDON D. WEBSTER

The city of Glasgow, formerly one of the largest industrial centres in the world, was once responsible for building about one-quarter of the world's railway locomotives. This was complemented by a massive urban railway network: the second largest in the UK. However, the Beeching Report of 1963 inevitably took its toll on Glasgow. This book examines the changing face of Glasgow's railways ever since that infamous report, starting with the period of rationalisation and industrial decline that followed. It also explores the revival enjoyed in the last few decades, with lines reopened and modern rolling stock introduced.

978 0 7524 9907 9

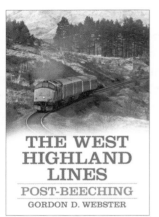

The West Highland Lines: Post-Beeching

GORDON D. WEBSTER

The railway lines of the West Highlands of Scotland are famous the world over for their illustrious history and unparalleled scenic beauty. Linking Glasgow with Oban, Fort William and Mallaig, they managed to survive the axe of Dr Beeching. With a detailed look at the routes, their workings and rolling stock since then, Webster examines how the West Highland network has gone on to prosper to the present day. Despite facing many challenges, the network retained its unique infrastructure in the modern age. Today the use of modern traction, together with the return of steam-hauled trains, has added yet another dimension to this wonderful scenic route.

978 0 7524 9706 8

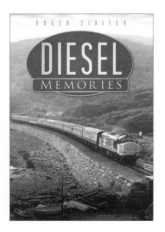

Diesel Memories

ROGER SIVITER

The advent of diesel on Britain's railways at the end of the age of steam meant the introduction of many locomotive designs from a variety of manufacturers. Some were highly successful and generated an enthusiastic following that continues today. Diesel Memories is a superb collection of black-and-white photographs, supported by Roger Siviter's informative research. In addition to the locomotives, there is an important photographic record of locations which have changed almost beyond recognition and of the railway infrastructure. This book will remind readers of a fascinating evolutionary period for Britain's railways.

978 0 7524 5245 6

Visit our website and discover thousands of other History Press books.

www.thehistorypress.co.uk